Symbols of Freedom

The Franklin Delano Roosevelt Memorial

Ted and Lola Schaefer

Heinemann Library
Chicago, Illinois

© 2006 Heinemann Library
a division of Reed Elsevier Inc.
Chicago, Illinois

Customer Service 888-454-2279

Visit our website at www.heinemannlibrary.com

Designed by Richard Parker and Mike Hogg Design
Illustrations by Jeff Edwards
Originated by Chroma Graphics (Overseas) Pte.Ltd.
Printed and bound in China by South China Printing Company

10 09 08 07 06
10 9 8 7 6 5 4 3 2 1

Library of Congress Cataloging-in-Publication Data
Schaefer, Ted, 1948-
 The Franklin Delano Roosevelt Memorial / Ted and Lola M. Schaefer.
    p. cm. -- (Symbols of freedom)
 Includes index.
 ISBN 1-4034-6661-0 (library binding-hardcover) -- ISBN 1-4034-6670-X (pbk.)
 1. Franklin Delano Roosevelt Memorial (Washington,D.C.)--Juvenile literature. 2. Roosevelt, Franklin D. (Franklin Delano), 1882-1945--Monuments--Washington (D.C)--Juvenile literature. 3. Washington (D.C.)--Buildings, structures, etc.--Juvenile literature. I. Schaefer, Lola M., 1950- II. Title. III. Series.
 F203.4.F73S33 2005
 975.3--dc22
                        2005002037

Acknowledgments
The publishers would like to thank the following for permission to reproduce photographs:
Corbis pp. 7, 9, 14, 19, pp. 8, 12, 15 (Bettman); Getty Images pp. 11 (Hulton Archive), 5 (News), 16 (Ted Thai/Time Life Pictures); Jill Birschbach/Harcourt Education Ltd pp. 4, 17, 18, 20, 21, 22, 23, 24, 25, 27, 28, 29; Peter Newark's Americana Library pp. 6, 10, 13.

Cover photograph of the Franklin Delano Roosevelt statue reproduced with permission of Jill Birschbach/Harcourt Education Ltd.

In recognition of the National Park Service Rangers who are always present at the memorials, offering general information and interpretative tours. We thank you!

Every effort has been made to contact copyright holders of any material reproduced in this book. Any omissions will be rectified in subsequent printings if notice is given to the publishers.

The publishers and authors have done their best to ensure the accuracy and currency of all the information in this book, however, they can accept no responsibility for any loss, injury, or inconvenience sustained as a result of information or advice contained in the book.

Some words are shown in bold, **like this**. You can find out what they mean by looking in the glossary.

Contents

The Franklin Delano
    Roosevelt Memorial 4
Franklin Delano Roosevelt 6
A Difficult Time 8
Return to Public Service 10
President Roosevelt 12
Remembering a President 14
Building a Memorial 16
First Room. 18
Second Room 20
Third Room 22
Fourth Room 24
Visiting the Memorial 26
Fact File *28*
Timeline *29*
Glossary *30*
More Books to Read *31*
Index *32*

The Franklin Delano Roosevelt Memorial

The Franklin Delano Roosevelt **Memorial** is in Washington, D.C. It is near the Potomac River and the Jefferson Memorial. Flowering trees make a beautiful setting.

The Franklin Delano Roosevelt Memorial remembers the 32nd president of the United States. Franklin D. Roosevelt was **elected** president four times. He led the country through hard times.

Franklin Delano Roosevelt

Franklin D. Roosevelt was born in 1882. As a young man, he wanted to serve the country. He wanted to be like his cousin, President Theodore Roosevelt, shown here.

Franklin D. Roosevelt was **elected** to the
New York Senate in 1910. Three years
later President Woodrow Wilson made
him Assistant Secretary of the U.S.
Navy Department.

A Difficult Time

In 1921 Franklin became ill with **polio**. He could not stand or walk on his own. At first he was weak and afraid.

Then Franklin started to use a wheelchair. After lots of hard work, he learned to stand again. He decided to return to **public service**.

Return to Public Service

In 1929, Franklin D. Roosevelt became **governor** of New York. At the same time, life in the United States became difficult. Banks closed. Businesses struggled.

Many Americans lost their jobs. Some people had no food to eat. Others lost their homes. This began a time known as the **Great Depression.**

President Roosevelt

Franklin D. Roosevelt became president in 1933. Right away, he started many **programs** to help the American people. But it would take time to fix the country's problems.

From 1941 to 1945, the United States fought in **World War II**. President Roosevelt was a strong leader. All Americans worked together with other countries and won the war.

Remembering a President

On April 12, 1945, President Roosevelt died.
Ten years later the U.S. Congress set up a
commission to plan and build a **memorial**
for him.

The commission found a good place for the memorial. They asked Lawrence Halprin to **design** it. He planned a memorial made of stone and **bronze**.

Building a Memorial

Waterfalls and pools were built in the **memorial**. **Sculptors** made **bronze** statues. Stonecutters carved famous words spoken by President Roosevelt. The memorial was completed in 1997.

The memorial tells the story of President Roosevelt's leadership. **Granite** walls form four outdoor rooms. Each room shows important events from one of his four **terms**.

The first room is full of hope. This **sculpture** shows Americans cheering Franklin D. Roosevelt on the day he became president. They believed he would make their lives better.

President Roosevelt met with many Americans. He listened to their problems and promised to work hard for them. His plan to help was called the New Deal.

Second Room

The second room is **grim**. Many problems still faced Americans. This **sculpture** shows men in a city standing in line, waiting for food.

Franklin D. Roosevelt was the first president
to speak to Americans on the radio. His words
gave them hope. These talks were called
"fireside chats."

Third Room

The third room is loud and rough, like war. Water crashes and splashes down rocks. Large **granite** stones tumble across the ground.

I HAVE SEEN WAR

I HAVE SEEN WAR ON LAND AND SEA. I HAVE SEEN
BLOOD RUNNING FROM THE WOUNDED... I HAVE
SEEN THE DEAD IN THE MUD. I HAVE SEEN CITIES
DESTROYED... I HAVE SEEN CHILDREN STARVING.
I HAVE SEEN THE AGONY OF MOTHERS AND WIVES.

I HATE WAR

In 1941, the United States joined **World War II**. Many Americans were afraid. This **sculpture** shows President Roosevelt as a calm and strong leader of the country.

Fourth Room

The fourth room is quiet and peaceful. President Roosevelt died early in his fourth **term**. This **sculpture** shows his funeral **procession**.

Many people **mourned** President Roosevelt's death. Their leader was gone. But his words carved on this wall remind us of the **freedoms** he wanted for all Americans.

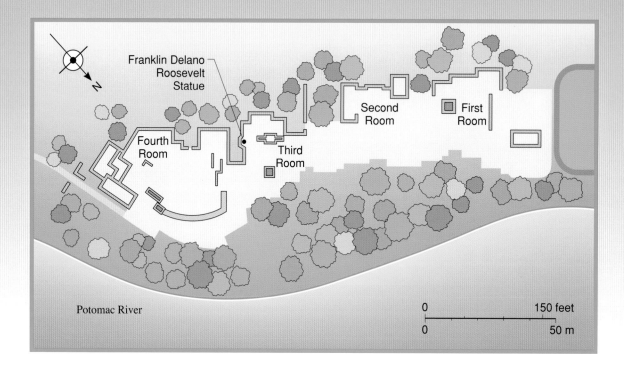

Franklin Delano
Roosevelt
Statue

Second
Room

First
Room

Fourth
Room

Third
Room

Potomac River

0   150 feet

0   50 m

Here is a map showing the Franklin Delano Roosevelt **Memorial** on the **National Mall**. When you visit think of President Roosevelt and what he did for the United States.

President Roosevelt started **programs** that changed the U.S. government. He led the country to protect **freedom** in **World War II**. Many Americans think he was a great president.

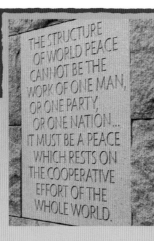

THE STRUCTURE OF WORLD PEACE CANNOT BE THE WORK OF ONE MAN, OR ONE PARTY, OR ONE NATION... IT MUST BE A PEACE WHICH RESTS ON THE COOPERATIVE EFFORT OF THE WHOLE WORLD.

Fact File

FDR Memorial

★ President Roosevelt had a black Scottish terrier named Fala who was always with him. He sat with the President in the Oval Office during important meetings. He traveled with the President in his private train car.

★ Franklin D. Roosevelt served more than twelve years as president of the United States. That was four **terms**. A term is four years. Since he died in 1945, President Roosevelt was unable to finish his fourth term.

★ It took 31,439 separate stone blocks to build the Franklin Delano Roosevelt **Memorial**. The heaviest stone weighed more than seven large elephants!

Timeline

FDR Memorial

* 1882   Franklin D. Roosevelt is born
* 1901–1909   Theodore Roosevelt is president of the United States
* 1921   Franklin D. Roosevelt is stricken with **polio** and cannot walk
* 1933   Franklin D. Roosevelt takes office as the 32nd president of the United States
* 1945   On April 12th President Roosevelt dies in Warm Springs, Georgia
* 1955   U.S. Congress sets up the Franklin Delano Roosevelt **Commission**
* 1974   Lawrence Halprin is chosen to **design** the Franklin Delano Roosevelt Memorial
* 1997   The Franklin Delano Roosevelt Memorial is dedicated

Glossary

brace object attached to another object, or to a body part, to hold it in place

bronze hard, reddish brown metal that is a mixture of copper and tin

commission group of people who meet to do a certain task or job

design draw the shape and style of something

elect choose someone or decide something by voting

freedom having the right to say, behave, or move about as you please

governor person who rules or governs a state

granite hard rock often used as a building material

Great Depression time during the 1930s when banks and businesses closed down and many people lost their jobs

grim gloomy; not very nice

memorial something that is built to help us remember a person, or event

mourn being very sad about someone who has died

National Mall large, park-like area of land in Washington, D.C. where museums and memorials are built

pledge make a promise

polio illness that can stop you being able to stand or walk. Polio mainly affects children.

procession group of people walking of driving along in line as part of a celebration, service, or parade

program schedule or plan for doing something

public service working in the government for the people

sculptor person who carves shapes out of stone, wood, metal, marble, or clay

sculpture something carved or shaped out of stone, wood, metal, marble, or clay

term period of time. The president of the United States serves a four-year term as president.

World War II war in which the United States, Great Britain, France, the Soviet Union, and other allied nations beat Germany, Italy, and Japan. The war began in 1939 and ended in 1945.

More Books to Read

An older reader can help you with these books:

Peduzzi, Kelli. *Shaping a President: Sculpting for the Roosevelt Memorial.* Brookfield, Conn.: Millbrook Press, 1997.

Phillips, Anne. *The Franklin Delano Roosevelt Memorial.* N.Y.: Children's Press, 2000.

Visiting the Memorial

The Franklin Delano Roosevelt Memorial is open every day of the year, except Christmas Day (December 25), 8:00 A.M. to midnight. Park rangers are present during these times to answer questions or give talks on the memorial.

To ask for a brochure and map of the Franklin Delano Roosevelt Memorial, write to this address:

National Park Service
900 Ohio Drive SW
Washington, D.C. 20024.

Index

bronze 15, 16

dedication 29

Fala (Scottish terrier) 23, 28
"fireside chats" 21
freedom 25, 27
funeral procession 25

Great Depression 11

Halprin, Lawrence 15, 29

leadership 13, 17, 23

memorial commission 14, 15, 29

New Deal 19

outdoor rooms 17–25

polio 8–9, 29
presidential terms 17, 28
programs 12, 27

Roosevelt, Franklin D. 5–10,
    12–14, 16, 17, 18-19, 21, 23,
    24–25, 26–27, 28, 29
Roosevelt, Theodore 6, 29

sculptures 16, 18, 20, 23, 24

visiting the Memorial 26–27, 31

Washington, D.C. 4
waterfalls and pools 16, 22
Wilson, Woodrow 7
words of Franklin D. Roosevelt 25
World War II 13, 23, 27